Guided Spelling™

First edition published 2009.

Guided Spelling is a trademark of Center for the Collaborative Classroom.

Center for the Collaborative Classroom
1001 Marina Village Parkway, Suite 110
Alameda, CA 94501
(800) 666-7270; fax: (510) 464-3670
collaborativeclassroom.org

ISBN-13: 978-1-59892-127-4
ISBN-10: 1-59892-127-4

Printed in Canada

2 3 4 5 6 7 8 9 10 11 MQB 26 25 24 23 22 21 20 19 18

Contents

Guided Spelling Lessons

Name:

_____

Short Vowels; Frequently Misspelled Words

NEW WORDS

____	*1. trunk	She keeps a spare tire in the trunk of her car.
____	*2. skin	Protect your skin with sunscreen when you are outside.
____	*3. knock	I will knock on the door when I arrive.
____	*4. nonfat	In nonfat milk, all the fat has been removed.
____	*5. pledge	A pledge is a promise.
____	*6. crops	The farmer's main crops were broccoli and lettuce.
____	*7. switches	We flipped the switches to shut off the power.
____	*8. thrill	What a thrill it was to ride the roller coaster!
____	9. twelve	We will eat lunch at twelve o'clock today.
____	10. sense	Owls have a very good sense of sight; they can see prey from far away.
____	11. know	I practiced my spelling words, and I know them all.
____	12. halfway	Let's each start from home and meet halfway.
____	13. something	He knew he had forgotten something.
____	14. you're	I see that you're finished.
____	15. couldn't	She couldn't open the jar's lid.

1. _____

2. _____

3. _____

4. _____

5. _____

6. _____

7. _____

8. _____

1. _____

2. _____

3. _____

4. _____

5. _____

6. _____

7. _____

8. _____

1. _____

2. _____

3. _____

4. _____

5. _____

6. _____

7. _____

8. _____

1. _____

2. _____

3. _____

4. _____

5. _____

6. _____

7. _____

8. _____

Doubling with Single-syllable Words; Frequently Misspelled Words

NEW WORDS

____	*1. trotting	The horses were trotting around the track.
____	*2. skidded	The player skidded into first base.
____	*3. swimmer	The swimmer made record time in the breaststroke.
____	*4. camping	The hikers are camping in the desert.
____	*5. muddy	The rain boots were muddy; they were covered with mud.
____	*6. printed	School menus are printed on recycled paper.
____	*7. fixing	The plumber was fixing the leaky faucet.
____	*8. misled	We were misled by the wrong directions and got lost.
____	9. thought	We thought it was a funny movie.
____	10. I'm	My parents know I'm going to visit my friend.
____	11. who's	I wonder who's in charge.
____	12. they've	I am surprised they've finished their work so quickly.
____	13. which	He considered which fruit to choose: an apricot or a banana.
____	14. sure	She was sure her answer was right.
____	15. whole	They ran the whole five-mile race.

REVIEW WORDS

____ *16. pledge

____ *17. knock

____ *18. crops

____ *19. nonfat

____ *20. thrill

____ *21. switches

____ 22. something

____ 23. sense

____ 24. you're

____ 25. halfway

Challenge Words

bushes, strength, flatten, jogging, trimming

Week 2, Day 1

1. _____ + _____ = _____

2. _____ + _____ = _____

3. _____

4. _____

5. _____ + _____ = _____

6. _____

7. _____

8. _____

1. _____ + _____ = _____

2. _____ + _____ = _____

3. _____

4. _____

5. _____

6. _____

7. _____ + _____ = _____

8. _____

9. _____

10. _____

_____

Name: _____

1. _____ + _____ = _____

2. _____ + _____ = _____

3. _____

4. _____

5. _____

6. _____

7. _____ + _____ = _____

8. _____

9. _____

10. _____

_____

1. _____ + _____ = _____

2. _____ + _____ = _____

3. _____

4. _____

5. _____

6. _____

7. _____ + _____ = _____

8. _____

9. _____

10. _____

_____

Long Vowels; Frequently Misspelled Words

NEW WORDS

___	*1. rays	The sun's rays came through the window.
___	*2. goals	The soccer team scored two goals during the game.
___	*3. preflight	Astronauts have many preflight tasks.
___	*4. twice	I fell twice while I was skating.
___	*5. airplane	The airplane landed on the runway and taxied to the gate.
___	*6. meatless	My cousin doesn't eat meat; all of his meals are meatless.
___	*7. cage	We keep the hamster in its cage.
___	*8. throw	The catcher will throw the ball to the pitcher.
___	9. unwrapped	He unwrapped his birthday gift.
___	10. o'clock	School begins at eight o'clock in the morning.
___	11. piece	She molded the piece of clay into a bowl.
___	12. paid	We paid for our tickets and went into the movie theater.
___	13. we'd	She thought we'd be there by noon.
___	14. that'll	He knows that'll be his last time at bat for the game.
___	15. their	They carried their camping gear in backpacks.

REVIEW WORDS

____ *16. muddy

____ *17. misled

____ *18. fixing

____ *19. skidded

____ *20. camping

____ *21. trotting

____ 22. I'm

____ 23. sure

____ 24. who's

____ 25. they've

Challenge Words

faith, beard, glow, throne, squeeze

Name: _____

1. _____

2. _____

3. _____

4. _____

5. _____

6. _____

7. _____

8. _____

1. _____

2. _____

3. _____

4. _____

5. _____

6. _____

7. _____

8. _____

9. _____

10. _____

_____

1. _____

2. _____

3. _____

4. _____

5. _____

6. _____

7. _____

8. _____

9. _____

10. _____

_____

1. _____

2. _____

3. _____

4. _____

5. _____

6. _____

7. _____

8. _____

9. _____

10. _____

_____

Polysyllabic Spelling

NEW WORDS

___	*1. intend	I intend to finish my homework before dinner.
___	*2. conflict	The group considered how to resolve the conflict.
___	*3. twenty	There were twenty books on the bookshelf.
___	*4. details	Pay attention to the details of the directions.
___	*5. shadow	The small mouse was hidden in the shadow of the plant.
___	*6. extremely	It was extremely hot today; it was over 100 degrees.
___	*7. deal	She will deal the cards to each player.
___	*8. low	They ran low on art supplies.
___	9. reach	Can you reach to the top shelf?
___	10. laid	She laid her head on the pillow and fell asleep.
___	11. tank	He fills the gas tank regularly.
___	12. hidden	We found a baby lizard hidden in the garden.
___	13. steel	The bridge was made of steel.
___	14. wide	The door was wide open.
___	15. broad	The road was flat and broad, with a lot of space to ride.

REVIEW WORDS

___ *16. airplane

___ *17. throw

___ *18. goals

___ *19. twice

___ *20. cage

___ *21. rays

___ 22. piece

___ 23. unwrapped

___ 24. we'd

___ 25. paid

Challenge Words

acre, ruin, countryside, museum, poetry

Name: _____

1. _____

2. _____

3. _____

4. _____

5. _____

6. _____

7. _____

8. _____

1. _____

2. _____

3. _____

4. _____

5. _____

6. _____

7. _____

8. _____

9. _____

10. _____

_____

Name: _____

1. _____

2. _____

3. _____

4. _____

5. _____

6. _____

7. _____

8. _____

9. _____

10. _____

_____

1. _____

2. _____

3. _____

4. _____

5. _____

6. _____

7. _____

8. _____

9. _____

10. _____

_____

Syllables with Schwas

NEW WORDS

___	*1. promise	If I promise to do something, I will do it.
___	*2. buffalo	The American buffalo is a large, hairy mammal.
___	*3. kitchen	They cooked and ate their meals in the kitchen.
___	*4. immediately	I was so hungry that I ate immediately.
___	*5. magnet	The magnet kept the photo on the refrigerator.
___	*6. opposite	The opposite of "enormous" is "tiny."
___	*7. succeed	He will try hard to succeed.
___	*8. cotton	Her shirt and pants are made out of cotton.
___	9. depth	The scientists will measure the depth of the lake.
___	10. slept	My dog always slept on my bed.
___	11. shopping	We went shopping for groceries.
___	12. bowl	She poured her cereal into the bowl.
___	13. advice	The teacher gave good advice about how to study.
___	14. roll	He will roll up his sleeping bag.
___	15. value	I value my pets; they mean a lot to me.

Name: _____

REVIEW WORDS

___ *16. twenty

___ *17. extremely

___ *18. details

___ *19. conflict

___ *20. low

___ *21. shadow

___ 22. wide

___ 23. hidden

___ 24. tank

___ 25. steel

Challenge Words

button, honesty, rocket, palm, elephant

1. _____

2. _____

3. _____

4. _____

5. _____

6. _____

7. _____

8. _____

1. _____

2. _____

3. _____

4. _____

5. _____

6. _____

7. _____

8. _____

9. _____

10. _____

_____

Name: _____

1. _____

2. _____

3. _____

4. _____

5. _____

6. _____

7. _____

8. _____

9. _____

10. _____

_____

1. _____

2. _____

3. _____

4. _____

5. _____

6. _____

7. _____

8. _____

9. _____

10. _____

_____

Week 6

Name: _____

Review of Weeks 1, 2, 3, and 4

Week 1

___ *1. skin

___ *2. pledge

___ *3. trunk

___ *4. knock

___ *5. switches

___ 6. couldn't

___ 7. twelve

___ 8. you're

___ 9. know

___ 10. sense

Week 2

___ *11. swimmer

___ *12. fixing

___ *13. muddy

___ *14. printed

___ *15. skidded

___ 16. thought

___ 17. whole

___ 18. they've

___ 19. which

___ 20. who's

Week 3

___ *21. preflight

___ *22. cage

___ *23. goals

___ *24. meatless

___ *25. twice

___ 26. o'clock

___ 27. that'll

___ 28. paid

___ 29. their

___ 30. unwrapped

continues

REVIEW WEEK WORDS (continued)

Week 4

___ *31. intend

___ *32. deal

___ *33. details

___ *34. extremely

___ *35. shadow

___ 36. laid

___ 37. reach

___ 38. steel

___ 39. broad

___ 40. hidden

Challenge Words

Week 2 flatten, bushes, strength, trimming, jogging

Week 3 glow, faith, squeeze, throne, beard

Week 4 ruin, museum, countryside, acre, poetry

Name: _____

1. _____

2. _____

3. _____

4. _____

5. _____

6. _____

7. _____

8. _____

9. _____

10. _____

11. _____

12. _____

13. _____

14. _____

15. _____

1. _____

The car skidded twice on Green Road, whitch was extremly muddy that day.

2. _____

At twelfe oclock sharp there was a loud knock at the door.

3. _____

The swimer intended to reech his training goles by September.

4. _____

Whose unwrapped the present that was hiden so carefully?

5. _____

I know your adding more detales to your paragraph.

Drop e Generalization

NEW WORDS

____	*1. requiring	The teacher will be requiring us to do daily homework.
____	*2. smoky	The air was smoky after the brush fire.
____	*3. preparing	She is preparing for the test by studying.
____	*4. trader	A North American fur trader would travel great distances by canoe.
____	*5. broken	The leg on the chair is broken.
____	*6. wisest	The owl is sometimes considered the wisest of birds.
____	*7. supposed to	We are supposed to brush our teeth at least twice a day.
____	*8. refusing	My dog was refusing to sit for a treat.
____	9. topic	The geography topic for this week is the mountain ranges of the western United States.
____	10. swimming	He will be doing a lot of swimming in this hot weather.
____	11. upstairs	The bedrooms of this house are upstairs.
____	12. attach	I will attach this light to my bike.
____	13. palace	The palace contained a hundred beautiful rooms.
____	14. glance	A glance is a quick look.
____	15. fence	The fence keeps our dog in our yard.

REVIEW WORDS

___ *16. opposite

___ *17. buffalo

___ *18. cotton

___ *19. immediately

___ *20. promise

___ 21. slept

___ 22. depth

___ 23. bowl

___ 24. shopping

___ 25. value

Challenge Words

meanwhile, holiday, excused, amazing, confusing

1. _____ + _____ = _____

2. _____ + _____ = _____

3. _____

4. _____

5. _____ + _____ = _____

6. _____

7. _____

8. _____

1. _____ + _____ = _____

2. _____ + _____ = _____

3. _____

4. _____

5. _____

6. _____

7. _____ + _____ = _____

8. _____

9. _____

10. _____

_____

Name: _____

1. _____ + _____ = _____

2. _____ + _____ = _____

3. _____

4. _____

5. _____

6. _____

7. _____ + _____ = _____

8. _____

9. _____

10. _____

_____

1. _____ + _____ = _____

2. _____ + _____ = _____

3. _____

4. _____

5. _____

6. _____

7. _____ + _____ = _____

8. _____

9. _____

10. _____

_____

Syllables with **r**-controlled Vowels

NEW WORDS

___	*1. concern	There is concern about a water shortage because of the drought.
___	*2. alarm	I got up when the alarm clock buzzed.
___	*3. border	I will add a red border to the quilt.
___	*4. dirty	The dirty laundry goes in the washing machine.
___	*5. misreported	The announcer misreported the accident because he did not interview the witnesses.
___	*6. surprising	It was surprising to see a crowd at the mall so early.
___	*7. prerecorded	The television show was prerecorded and shown at a later time.
___	*8. unexplored	Much of Antarctica was unexplored by humans.
___	9. chapter	I'm on the second chapter of the adventure book.
___	10. knees	She scraped her knees playing volleyball.
___	11. belong	Does this pencil belong to you?
___	12. collect	My sister likes to collect shells at the beach.
___	13. staring	The owl was staring at the mouse without even blinking.
___	14. ought	We ought to leave now to arrive at the movie on time.
___	15. fought	They fought for their right to vote.

REVIEW WORDS

___ *16. requiring

___ *17. supposed to

___ *18. wisest

___ *19. preparing

___ *20. trader

___ 21. palace

___ 22. attach

___ 23. glance

___ 24. swimming

___ 25. topic

Challenge Words

conquer, fortune, germs, margin, urge

1. _____

2. _____

3. _____

4. _____

5. _____

6. _____

7. _____

8. _____

1. _____

2. _____

3. _____

4. _____

5. _____

6. _____

7. _____

8. _____

9. _____

10. _____

_____

1. _____

2. _____

3. _____

4. _____

5. _____

6. _____

7. _____

8. _____

9. _____

10. _____

_____

1. _____

2. _____

3. _____

4. _____

5. _____

6. _____

7. _____

8. _____

9. _____

10. _____

_____

Change **y** to **i** Generalization

NEW WORDS

___	*1. satisfied	That was a delicious meal; I am satisfied.
___	*2. applied	My sister has applied for college.
___	*3. applying	He will be applying for an internship at that company this summer.
___	*4. centuries	Many of the redwood trees have been growing for centuries.
___	*5. colonial	In American colonial times, much of the furniture was handmade.
___	*6. relying	I am relying on you to tell the truth.
___	*7. armies	Ant armies swarmed the picnic area.
___	*8. beautiful	The rose bushes are beautiful in full bloom.
___	9. paper	We used construction paper for the art project.
___	10. visit	She will visit her cousins this weekend.
___	11. wagon	The toddlers pulled the red wagon around the yard.
___	12. describing	He was describing the book to his classmates.
___	13. wore	He wore a dress shirt to the concert.
___	14. tongue	We taste different flavors with different parts of our tongue.
___	15. dozen	She bought a dozen eggs at the market.

REVIEW WORDS

___ *16. border

___ *17. dirty

___ *18. concern

___ *19. prerecorded

___ *20. misreported

___ 21. fought

___ 22. chapter

___ 23. collect

___ 24. belong

___ 25. knees

Challenge Words

silliest, warmth, cleanliness, denied, tennis

Name: _____

1. _____ + _____ = _____

2. _____ + _____ = _____

3. _____

4. _____

5. _____ + _____ = _____

6. _____

7. _____

8. _____

1. _____ + _____ = _____

2. _____ + _____ = _____

3. _____

4. _____

5. _____

6. _____

7. _____ + _____ = _____

8. _____

9. _____

10. _____

_____

Name: _____

1. _____ + _____ = _____

2. _____ + _____ = _____

3. _____

4. _____

5. _____

6. _____

7. _____ + _____ = _____

8. _____

9. _____

10. _____

_____

1. _____ + _____ = _____

2. _____ + _____ = _____

3. _____

4. _____

5. _____

6. _____

7. _____ + _____ = _____

8. _____

9. _____

10. _____

_____

Name:
_____

Other Vowel Digraphs

NEW WORDS

___	*1. smoother	They sanded the wood to make it smoother.
___	*2. football	They were playing touch football.
___	*3. county	The largest town in the county is often the county seat.
___	*4. choice	The menu offered a wide choice of dishes.
___	*5. raw	Uncooked meat is raw meat.
___	*6. flew	The blue jay flew into the pine tree.
___	*7. introduce	I'd like to introduce you to my friend.
___	*8. uncrowded	The store was surprisingly uncrowded.
___	9. evening	The crickets began to chirp in the evening.
___	10. pocket	He kept his keys in his pocket.
___	11. hiring	The store is hiring new employees for the summer.
___	12. perhaps	He hasn't written to me; perhaps he lost my address.
___	13. enemies	The two teams were opponents, not enemies.
___	14. route	We will take the route over the mountains.
___	15. system	There is a large bus system in our community; people can take a bus to many places.

REVIEW WORDS

___ *16. relying

___ *17. beautiful

___ *18. armies

___ *19. satisfied

___ *20. centuries

___ *21. applied

___ 22. paper

___ 23. dozen

___ 24. wore

___ 25. wagon

Challenge Words

astronaut, coiled, powder, cargo, squawking

1. _____

2. _____

3. _____

4. _____

5. _____

6. _____

7. _____

8. _____

1. _____

2. _____

3. _____

4. _____

5. _____

6. _____

7. _____

8. _____

9. _____

10. _____

_____

Name: _____

1. _____

2. _____

3. _____

4. _____

5. _____

6. _____

7. _____

8. _____

9. _____

10. _____

_____

1. _____

2. _____

3. _____

4. _____

5. _____

6. _____

7. _____

8. _____

9. _____

10. _____

_____

Possessive Nouns and Pronouns

NEW WORDS

____	*1. giant's	Beyond the wall was a fierce giant. The giant's head was huge.
____	*2. giants'	Giants were fighting. The giants' battle was heard throughout the kingdom.
____	*3. children's	The children's section of the library is very popular.
____	*4. its	A monarch butterfly is noticeable because its wings are black and orange.
____	*5. sisters'	The three daughters all had bikes. The sisters' bicycles were lined up in front of the house.
____	*6. sister's	Her oldest sister's backpack was left on the table.
____	*7. it's	Today is beautiful because it's sunny and warm.
____	*8. nurses'	Nurses' uniforms used to be white.
____	9. rather	I'd rather go swimming than play tennis.
____	10. defining	We used both context and the dictionary for defining the words.
____	11. farther	Our classroom is farther from the office than yours.
____	12. replying	I will be replying to the letter.
____	13. announce	They will announce the winner tonight.
____	14. character	Her favorite character in the book was the hero.
____	15. stomach	The human stomach can digest many types of food.

REVIEW WORDS

___ *16. raw

___ *17. county

___ *18. football

___ *19. uncrowded

___ *20. smoother

___ *21. flew

___ 22. pocket

___ 23. perhaps

___ 24. system

___ 25. route

Challenge Words

seize, assignment, diagram, interfered, cauliflower

Name: _____

1. _____

2. _____

3. _____

4. _____

5. _____

6. _____

7. _____

8. _____

1. _____

2. _____

3. _____

4. _____

5. _____

6. _____

7. _____

8. _____

9. _____

10. _____

_____

Name: _____

1. _____

2. _____

3. _____

4. _____

5. _____

6. _____

7. _____

8. _____

9. _____

10. _____

_____

1. _____

2. _____

3. _____

4. _____

5. _____

6. _____

7. _____

8. _____

9. _____

10. _____

_____

Week 12

Review of Weeks 5, 7, 8, 9, and 10

Week 5

___ *1. magnet   ___ *6. promise

___ *2. succeed   ___ 7. value

___ *3. kitchen   ___ 8. roll

___ *4. opposite   ___ 9. depth

___ *5. immediately   ___ 10. advice

Week 7

___ *11. broken   ___ 16. attach

___ *12. refusing   ___ 17. topic

___ *13. smoky   ___ 18. fence

___ *14. supposed to   ___ 19. glance

___ *15. preparing   ___ 20. upstairs

Week 8

___ *21. dirty   ___ *26. alarm

___ *22. border   ___ 27. staring

___ *23. concern   ___ 28. chapter

___ *24. unexplored   ___ 29. collect

___ *25. surprising   ___ 30. ought

continues

REVIEW WEEK WORDS (continued)

Week 9

____ *31. centuries

____ *32. beautiful

____ *33. colonial

____ *34. applying

____ *35. satisfied

____ 36. tongue

____ 37. visit

____ 38. dozen

____ 39. describing

____ 40. wore

Week 10

____ *41. choice

____ *42. smoother

____ *43. introduce

____ *44. uncrowded

____ *45. flew

____ *46. county

____ 47. hiring

____ 48. evening

____ 49. route

____ 50. enemies

Challenge Words

Week 5 button, honesty, rocket, palm, elephant

Week 7 meanwhile, excused, confusing, amazing, holiday

Week 8 conquer, germs, margin, urge, fortune

Week 9 tennis, silliest, denied, warmth, cleanliness

Week 10 powder, coiled, cargo, squawking, astronaut

Name: _____

1. _____

2. _____

3. _____

4. _____

5. _____

6. _____

7. _____

8. _____

9. _____

10. _____

11. _____

12. _____

13. _____

14. _____

15. _____

Name: _____

1. _____

   Pioneers in unexplorred territory regarded a broken wheel with concirn.

2. _____

   The county had had its name for centurys.

3. _____

   One evening during their visit to the country, they sat on the fense

   _____

   and gazed at a beautyful sunset.

4. _____

   She's describing how a magnit attracts the oppasite end of another magnut.

5. _____

   The alarm rang in the smokey kitchin when he burned the roles.

Syllables -*tion* and -*sion*

NEW WORDS

___	*1. protection	Seatbelts protect us, and their protection makes us safer.
___	*2. division	This math problem requires division, so you will have to divide.
___	*3. operation	It's an unusually long operation when the doctors have to operate for seven hours.
___	*4. expression	She likes to express herself with the expression "OK!"
___	*5. permission	When their parents permit them to go to the park, they give permission.
___	*6. suggestion	When you suggest a plan, you are making a suggestion.
___	*7. motionless	While playing hide-and-seek, the girl tried to remain motionless so no one would find her.
___	*8. instructions	When your teachers give instructions, they instruct you.
___	9. degrees	It is only 30 degrees outside!
___	10. furry	My mother complains that our furry cat sheds all over the rug.
___	11. hungrier	"I'm hungrier than a bear!" my brother exaggerated.
___	12. background	In the background of the photo were snow-capped mountains.
___	13. captain's	Following the captain's orders, the men lowered the mainsail.

continues

NEW WORDS (continued)

____ 14. earn   On Fridays I babysit for my cousin to earn some spending money.

____ 15. daughter   The woman and her young daughter held hands as they walked to the park.

REVIEW WORDS

____ *16. children's

____ *17. giant's

____ *18. its

____ *19. nurses'

____ *20. giants'

____ 21. stomach

____ 22. rather

____ 23. announce

____ 24. farther

____ 25. defining

Challenge Words

possessions, protein, sword, destruction, expedition

1. _____

2. _____

3. _____

4. _____

5. _____

6. _____

7. _____

8. _____

1. _____

2. _____

3. _____

4. _____

5. _____

6. _____

7. _____

8. _____

9. _____

10. _____

_____

Name: _____

1. _____

2. _____

3. _____

4. _____

5. _____

6. _____

7. _____

8. _____

9. _____

10. _____

_____

1. _____

2. _____

3. _____

4. _____

5. _____

6. _____

7. _____

8. _____

9. _____

10. _____

_____

Syllables Ending in Consonant-**l-e** and Consonant-**a-l**

NEW WORDS

___	*1. gentle	He was a gentle dog who never even barked.
___	*2. capital	Begin the name of your capital city with a capital letter.
___	*3. metal	Sterling silver is one type of metal used to make jewelry.
___	*4. article	My sister wrote an article for the school newspaper.
___	*5. hospital	My dad is working as a nurse at the hospital.
___	*6. minerals	She took a daily dose of extra vitamins and minerals.
___	*7. medical	There are many jobs in the medical profession, including doctors, nurses, and technicians, to name just a few.
___	*8. muscles	The athlete soaked in a hot bath to ease her aching muscles.
___	9. extra	They saved the extra food for the next day.
___	10. sleepiest	Even the sleepiest child woke up when their dad came home.
___	11. discount	The store owner is my uncle's friend, so he gave us a discount.
___	12. yours	I found my notebook in my backpack, but I don't see yours.
___	13. dictionary	She likes to look at the illustrations in the dictionary.
___	14. double	He tied a double knot in his shoelaces.
___	15. camel	The camel is an important animal for many desert nomads.

REVIEW WORDS

____ *16. permission

____ *17. instructions

____ *18. protection

____ *19. division

____ *20. suggestion

____ *21. expression

____ 22. background

____ 23. earn

____ 24. hungrier

____ 25. furry

Challenge Words

mammal, sweaty, startled, initials, pupil

Name: _____

1. _____

2. _____

3. _____

4. _____

5. _____

6. _____

7. _____

8. _____

1. _____

2. _____

3. _____

4. _____

5. _____

6. _____

7. _____

8. _____

9. _____

10. _____

_____

Name: _____

1. _____

2. _____

3. _____

4. _____

5. _____

6. _____

7. _____

8. _____

9. _____

10. _____

_____

1. _____

2. _____

3. _____

4. _____

5. _____

6. _____

7. _____

8. _____

9. _____

10. _____

_____

Week 15

Name:
_____

Syllables with *-ive*, *-ture*, and *-age*

NEW WORDS

___	*1. expensive	The boy could not afford the game because it was too expensive.
___	*2. furniture	My grandma's house is full of old furniture.
___	*3. advantage	The other team had an advantage because they had one more player.
___	*4. relatives	I have more relatives on my mom's side than on my dad's.
___	*5. capturing	The juggler was capturing my brother's attention.
___	*6. damaged	My mother sent the new chair back because it was damaged.
___	*7. courage	You have to have a lot of courage to do rock climbing.
___	*8. tomorrow	I'm going to see my friend tomorrow.
___	9. camera	I forgot to get batteries for my camera!
___	10. royal	When the royal coach passed by, everyone tried to get a glimpse of the queen.
___	11. husband's	Her husband's family had lived in the town for three generations.
___	12. prevention	We hope that fire prevention programs will motivate everyone to prevent fires.
___	13. equal	The twins are of equal height.
___	14. honey	Honey and maple syrup are both sweeteners.
___	15. turkey	A wild turkey can fly a short distance.

REVIEW WORDS

___ *16. capital

___ *17. minerals

___ *18. muscles

___ *19. medical

___ *20. metal

___ *21. gentle

___ 22. double

___ 23. camel

___ 24. extra

___ 25. sleepiest

Challenge Words

literature, sewing, voyage, mixture, locomotive

1. _____

2. _____

3. _____

4. _____

5. _____

6. _____

7. _____

8. _____

1. _____

2. _____

3. _____

4. _____

5. _____

6. _____

7. _____

8. _____

9. _____

10. _____

_____

Name:
_____

1. _____

2. _____

3. _____

4. _____

5. _____

6. _____

7. _____

8. _____

9. _____

10. _____

_____

1. _____

2. _____

3. _____

4. _____

5. _____

6. _____

7. _____

8. _____

9. _____

10. _____

_____

Week 16

Name:
_____

Word Parts -*able* and -*ible*

NEW WORDS

___	*1. acceptable	It's acceptable to read quietly when you finish your test.
___	*2. responsibly	The teenager was careful to drive responsibly so her parents would allow her to use the car.
___	*3. valuable	Although it seems like an ordinary object, the teapot is very valuable to my mother.
___	*4. excitable	When my little brother plays with his friends, he is the most excitable of all.
___	*5. horrible	He had a horrible cold that kept him in bed for several days.
___	*6. reliable	The reliable old refrigerator finally quit working.
___	*7. noticeable	There was a noticeable smudge on the windowpane.
___	*8. comfortable	I love to lie on that couch because it's so comfortable.
___	9. forth	The baby swung back and forth and laughed with delight.
___	10. hers	When I looked closely at the backpack, I saw it was hers.
___	11. explanation	The book provided an explanation of gravity.
___	12. normal	After two days, her temperature returned to normal.
___	13. adventure	When we set off on the hiking trail without a map, my dad said, "This will be an adventure!"
___	14. tough	He had a tough time his first year away from home.
___	15. sorry	I am so sorry if I hurt your feelings.

REVIEW WORDS

___ *16. advantage

___ *17. courage

___ *18. furniture

___ *19. expensive

___ *20. capturing

___ 21. royal

___ 22. turkey

___ 23. husband's

___ 24. honey

___ 25. prevention

Challenge Words

irresponsible, miserable, worms, remarkable, incredible

1. _____

2. _____

3. _____

4. _____

5. _____

6. _____

7. _____

8. _____

1. _____

2. _____

3. _____

4. _____

5. _____

6. _____

7. _____

8. _____

9. _____

10. _____

_____

1. _____

2. _____

3. _____

4. _____

5. _____

6. _____

7. _____

8. _____

9. _____

10. _____

_____

1. _____

2. _____

3. _____

4. _____

5. _____

6. _____

7. _____

8. _____

9. _____

10. _____

_____

Name:

_____

Syllable *-ous* and Suffix *-ly*

NEW WORDS

___ *1. tremendous   A tremendous thunderclap followed the flash of lightning.

___ *2. proudly   "You played a great game!" her parents said proudly.

___ *3. easily   She is recovering from her illness, but still tires easily.

___ *4. curious   I'm curious to see whether the new baby looks like his mom or his dad.

___ *5. tightly   The child held tightly to his father's hand.

___ *6. serious   She is a serious student, but she also likes to have fun with her friends.

___ *7. truly   The letter was signed, "Very truly yours."

___ *8. actually   My uncle thought I was nine, but actually I am ten.

___ 9. orange   Please pass the orange juice.

___ 10. situation   Broken glass on the playground created a dangerous situation.

___ 11. signal   "Don't forget to use your turn signal," my dad reminded my brother.

___ 12. detective   The detective questioned the suspect about the clues he'd found.

___ 13. reusable   Many people prefer cloth napkins to paper napkins because they are reusable and don't have to be thrown away.

___ 14. calm   My teacher is always calm; she never gets angry.

___ 15. journey   The cross-country journey meant many long days in the car.

REVIEW WORDS

___ *16. excitable

___ *17. responsibly

___ *18. noticeable

___ *19. reliable

___*20. acceptable

___ 21. normal

___ 22. forth

___ 23. sorry

___ 24. hers

___ 25. adventure

Challenge Words

cleverly, journal, mildly, splendidly, cruelly

Name: _____

1. _____

2. _____

3. _____

4. _____

5. _____

6. _____

7. _____

8. _____

1. _____

2. _____

3. _____

4. _____

5. _____

6. _____

7. _____

8. _____

9. _____

10. _____

_____

Name: _____

1. _____

2. _____

3. _____

4. _____

5. _____

6. _____

7. _____

8. _____

9. _____

10. _____

_____

1. _____

2. _____

3. _____

4. _____

5. _____

6. _____

7. _____

8. _____

9. _____

10. _____

_____

Review of Weeks 11, 13, 14, 15, and 16

Week 11

___ *1. its (*Its fur is gray.*)

___ *2. sister's (*my sister's backpack*)

___ *3. sisters' (*two sisters' faces*)

___ *4. it's (*It's hot.*)

___ *5. children's

___ 6. replying

___ 7. defining

___ 8. character

___ 9. stomach

___ 10. announce

Week 13

___ *11. division

___ *12. suggestion

___ *13. motionless

___ *14. operation

___ *15. permission

___ 16. captain's (*captain's ship*)

___ 17. daughter

___ 18. earn

___ 19. degrees

___ 20. hungrier

Week 14

___ *21. muscles

___ *22. capital

___ *23. gentle

___ *24. hospital

___ *25. article

___ 26. dictionary

___ 27. sleepiest

___ 28. yours

___ 29. discount

___ 30. double

continues

REVIEW WEEK WORDS (continued)

Week 15

____ *31. courage

____ *32. relatives

____ *33. expensive

____ *34. tomorrow

____ *35. damaged

____ *36. furniture

____ 37. turkey

____ 38. royal

____ 39. camera

____ 40. equal

Week 16

____ *41. excitable

____ *42. responsibly

____ *43. noticeable

____ *44. comfortable

____ *45. horrible

____ *46. valuable

____ 47. forth

____ 48. sorry

____ 49. tough

____ 50. explanation

Challenge Words

Week 11 diagram, seize, assignment, interfered, cauliflower

Week 13 possessions, sword, protein, destruction, expedition

Week 14 startled, sweaty, mammal, pupil, initials

Week 15 literature, sewing, mixture, locomotive, voyage

Week 16 irresponsible, incredible, miserable, worms, remarkable

Name: _____

1. _____

2. _____

3. _____

4. _____

5. _____

6. _____

7. _____

8. _____

9. _____

10. _____

11. _____

12. _____

13. _____

14. _____

15. _____

1. _____

The two sister's dog was furry and adorable, but also very excitable.

2. _____

Tomorow the childrens' relative's will arrive for a visit.

3. _____

The dictionery is a valueable tool for difining difficult words.

4. _____

My sisters responsablely asked our parents' permision to go to

_____

the discount store.

5. _____

This artical contains the explanation of the knee operasion.

Syllables with -ant and -ent

NEW WORDS

____ *1. independent — The American colonies declared themselves independent in 1776.

____ *2. servant — When she first arrived in the United States, my grandmother worked as a servant.

____ *3. excellent — His handwriting is excellent.

____ *4. pleasant — A pleasant smell wafted up from the kitchen.

____ *5. silent — "Please take out a book for silent reading time," our teacher said.

____ *6. present, present — The class will present a farewell present to their teacher.

____ *7. accidentally — I accidentally dropped my pencil, and now I can't find it.

____ *8. content, content — She was content with the content of her new book about oceans.

____ 9. disposable — They used disposable cups on the picnic.

____ 10. needle — To sew on a button, you need a needle and thread.

____ 11. marriage — So far their marriage has lasted more than 50 years.

____ 12. reasonable — The traffic moved along at a reasonable rate, and we arrived on time.

____ 13. enormous — At the zoo, we saw enormous elephants and tiny baby chimpanzees.

____ 14. remove — My mother can remove that splinter for you.

____ 15. improve — I know I need to improve my handwriting.

REVIEW WORDS

____ *16. tightly

____ *17. easily

____ *18. truly

____ *19. curious

____ *20. tremendous

____ 21. reusable

____ 22. situation

____ 23. signal

____ 24. calm

____ 25. detective

Challenge Words

proficient, pearl, opponent, reluctant, resident

Name: _____

1. _____

2. _____

3. _____

4. _____

5. _____

6. _____

7. _____

8. _____

1. _____

2. _____

3. _____

4. _____

5. _____

6. _____

7. _____

8. _____

9. _____

10. _____

_____

1. _____

2. _____

3. _____

4. _____

5. _____

6. _____

7. _____

8. _____

9. _____

10. _____

_____

1. _____

2. _____

3. _____

4. _____

5. _____

6. _____

7. _____

8. _____

9. _____

10. _____

_____

Week 20

Syllables with -*ance* and -*ence*

NEW WORDS

____	*1. difference	It doesn't make any difference to me whether we leave in the morning or after lunch.
____	*2. distance	The distance between our house and my school is about six blocks.
____	*3. importance	They studied the importance of nutrition to growth.
____	*4. experience	Going to the aquarium with my class was a wonderful experience.
____	*5. sentence	The first sentence of the story was dramatic.
____	*6. performance	During the assembly, we saw a performance by local musicians.
____	*7. balance	The gymnast did a cartwheel on the balance beam.
____	*8. table of contents	After I finished my research report, I had to create a table of contents.
____	9. whisper	Please don't whisper during the movie.
____	10. garbage	One of my chores is to put the garbage out every Tuesday night.
____	11. sensible	Going to bed early the night before the long trip was a sensible decision.
____	12. peacefully	The cat and her kittens were sleeping peacefully.
____	13. assistants	The coach's two assistants helped the players run through some drills.

continues

NEW WORDS (continued)

___ 14. review   She wanted to review her vocabulary words before the quiz.

___ 15. mirror   The driver checked the rearview mirror before backing up.

REVIEW WORDS

___ *16. accidentally

___ *17. content (2)

___ *18. servant

___ *19. pleasant

___ *20. present (2)

___ 21. disposable

___ 22. improve

___ 23. needle

___ 24. remove

___ 25. enormous

Challenge Words

convenience, allegiance, persistence, elsewhere, violence

1. _____

2. _____

3. _____

4. _____

5. _____

6. _____

7. _____

8. _____

1. _____

2. _____

3. _____

4. _____

5. _____

6. _____

7. _____

8. _____

9. _____

10. _____

_____

Name: _____

1. _____

2. _____

3. _____

4. _____

5. _____

6. _____

7. _____

8. _____

9. _____

10. _____

_____

1. _____

2. _____

3. _____

4. _____

5. _____

6. _____

7. _____

8. _____

9. _____

10. _____

_____

Latin Roots *port* and *uni*

NEW WORDS

___ *1. port — At a port, ships unload cargo carried from distant places.

___ *2. transport — Trucks transport large quantities of fruits and vegetables from farms to stores.

___ *3. support — My dad offered his mother his arm as support when they went for a walk.

___ *4. opportunity — Next year we'll have the opportunity to study a foreign language.

___ *5. uniform — When a school has a uniform, all the students wear one style of outfit.

___ *6. united — The colonies united to become one country. They joined together into one nation.

___ *7. unit — An inch is one unit of measure.

___ *8. union — The thirteen colonies joined together to become a union—one country.

___ 9. welcome — Our teacher asked us to help the new student feel welcome.

___ 10. breakable — I need to be careful moving this vase because it's very breakable!

___ 11. painlessly — The nurse wished she could give shots painlessly.

___ 12. absent — The most common reason for being absent is illness.

___ 13. ambulance — Driving an ambulance takes skill and bravery.

continues

Name: _____

NEW WORDS (continued)

____ 14. steady   When I was learning to ride a bike, the hardest part was keeping it steady.

____ 15. pattern   They used a pattern to cut out intricate snowflakes.

REVIEW WORDS

____ *16. sentence

____ *17. performance

____ *18. distance

____ *19. table of contents

____ *20. experience

____ 21. garbage

____ 22. whisper

____ 23. assistants

____ 24. sensible

____ 25. peacefully

Challenge Words

imported, thread, unison, frontier, appreciate

Name: _____

1. _____

2. _____

3. _____

4. _____

5. _____

6. _____

7. _____

8. _____

1. _____

2. _____

3. _____

4. _____

5. _____

6. _____

7. _____

8. _____

9. _____

10. _____

_____

Name: _____

1. _____

2. _____

3. _____

4. _____

5. _____

6. _____

7. _____

8. _____

9. _____

10. _____

_____

1. _____

2. _____

3. _____

4. _____

5. _____

6. _____

7. _____

8. _____

9. _____

10. _____

_____

Name: _____

Suffixes That Mean *a person who* or *a thing that*

NEW WORDS

___ *1. manager   The store's manager worked long hours.

___ *2. sailor   Being a sailor on a whaling ship was a dangerous job.

___ *3. musician   My brother plays the guitar and hopes to be a professional musician.

___ *4. engineer   An engineer was called in when the building collapsed.

___ *5. superintendent   The superintendent visited every school monthly.

___ *6. artistic   Painting, drawing, music, and dance are all forms of artistic expression.

___ *7. trainer   The trainer feeds fish to the dolphins when they learn a new trick.

___ *8. fashion   Fashion changes so quickly that it's hard to keep up.

___ 9. surrounded   Beautiful mountains surrounded the small community.

___ 10. properly   His mother told him to dress properly for the occasion.

___ 11. innocent   The lawyer convinced the jury that her client was innocent.

___ 12. attendance   The wedding invitation began, "Your attendance is requested at the wedding."

___ 13. reporter   The job of a reporter is to gather facts and present them in an unbiased way.

continues

NEW WORDS (continued)

____ 14. tear, tear   The tear in her costume brought a tear to her eye.

____ 15. mouse   The mouse learned to run a complicated maze.

REVIEW WORDS

____ *16. opportunity

____ *17. port

____ *18. union

____ *19. unit

____ *20. transport

____ 21. welcome

____ 22. painlessly

____ 23. breakable

____ 24. pattern

____ 25. ambulance

Challenge Words

companion, lawyer, physician, governor, senator

Name: _____

1. _____

2. _____

3. _____

4. _____

5. _____

6. _____

7. _____

8. _____

1. _____

2. _____

3. _____

4. _____

5. _____

6. _____

7. _____

8. _____

9. _____

10. _____

_____

Name: _____

1. _____

2. _____

3. _____

4. _____

5. _____

6. _____

7. _____

8. _____

9. _____

10. _____

_____

1. _____

2. _____

3. _____

4. _____

5. _____

6. _____

7. _____

8. _____

9. _____

10. _____

_____

Week 23

Name: _____

Greek and Latin Roots

NEW WORDS

____ *1. particles   Particles are very small pieces.

____ *2. apart   The puzzle pieces came apart easily.

____ *3. department   A department is part of a store or office.

____ *4. partly   If you've partly done your job, you've done some pieces or parts of it.

____ *5. medicine   You need a doctor's prescription to get that medicine.

____ *6. microscope   With a microscope, we can see very small objects.

____ *7. telephone   The telephone was invented by Alexander Graham Bell.

____ *8. photograph   The old photograph of my mom's grandparents sits on her dresser.

____ 9. effortless   The professional tennis player made serving the ball look effortless.

____ 10. immigrant   An immigrant is a person who leaves one country to live in another country.

____ 11. conference   The teacher had a writing conference with each student.

____ 12. universe   Scientists send out space probes and satellites to gather information about the universe.

____ 13. computer   She sat down at her computer to finish her assignment.

continues

NEW WORDS (continued)

____ 14. layer   Whales have a layer of fat, called *blubber*, to keep them warm.

____ 15. quarter   The quarter coin is worth one-fourth of a dollar.

REVIEW WORDS

____ *16. sailor

____ *17. musician

____ *18. trainer

____ *19. fashion

____ *20. artistic

____ *21. manager

____ 22. reporter

____ 23. properly

____ 24. mouse

____ 25. attendance

Challenge Words

ghost, saxophone, participate, medication, telegraph

Name: _____

1. _____

2. _____

3. _____

4. _____

5. _____

6. _____

7. _____

8. _____

1. _____

2. _____

3. _____

4. _____

5. _____

6. _____

7. _____

8. _____

9. _____

10. _____

_____

Name: _____

1. _____

2. _____

3. _____

4. _____

5. _____

6. _____

7. _____

8. _____

9. _____

10. _____

_____

1. _____

2. _____

3. _____

4. _____

5. _____

6. _____

7. _____

8. _____

9. _____

10. _____

_____

Week 24

Name: _____

Review of Weeks 17, 19, 20, 21, and 22

Week 17

____ *1. truly

____ *2. actually

____ *3. curious

____ *4. easily

____ *5. serious

____ *6. proudly

____ 7. calm

____ 8. orange

____ 9. journey

____ 10. situation

Week 19

____ *11. accidentally

____ *12. silent

____ *13. excellent

____ *14. pleasant

____ *15. independent

____ 16. marriage

____ 17. disposable

____ 18. improve

____ 19. reasonable

____ 20. enormous

Week 20

____ *21. experience

____ *22. difference

____ *23. balance

____ *24. distance

____ *25. importance

____ *26. performance

____ 27. peacefully

____ 28. mirror

____ 29. sensible

____ 30. review

continues

REVIEW WEEK WORDS (*continued*)

Week 21

___ *31. union

___ *32. uniform

___ *33. support

___ *34. united

___ *35. opportunity

___ 36. absent

___ 37. breakable

___ 38. ambulance

___ 39. painlessly

___ 40. steady

Week 22

___ *41. musician

___ *42. manager

___ *43. superintendent

___ *44. sailor

___ *45. fashion

___ *46. engineer

___ 47. tear (2)

___ 48. innocent

___ 49. attendance

___ 50. surrounded

Challenge Words

Week 17 cruelly, journal, cleverly, mildly, splendidly

Week 19 opponent, resident, pearl, reluctant, proficient

Week 20 allegiance, elsewhere, violence, persistence, convenience

Week 21 thread, frontier, unison, appreciate, imported

Week 22 senator, lawyer, physician, companion, governor

Name: _____

1. _____

2. _____

3. _____

4. _____

5. _____

6. _____

7. _____

8. _____

9. _____

10. _____

11. _____

12. _____

13. _____

14. _____

15. _____

Name:

1. _____

The students proudly displayed their excelent artistic work.

2. _____

The last syllable must often be memorized, as in *independant*, *silent*,

accident, difference, experiance, balence, and disposable.

3. _____

The musicans were surounded by swirling dancers.

4. _____

His grandmother advised him to be serous, sensable, and curious on his

juorney through life.

Words with Prefixes

NEW WORDS

___	*1. forearm	Your forearm is the part of your arm from your elbow to your hand.
___	*2. subzero	A subzero temperature is one that is below zero degrees on a thermometer.
___	*3. semisweet	We used semisweet chocolate chips in the cookies.
___	*4. injustice	Being sent to prison without a trial is an injustice.
___	*5. supermarket	A supermarket is larger than a small market and sells a wide variety of goods.
___	*6. cooperating	The parents were amazed at the way the small groups were cooperating.
___	*7. encode	To encode a message is to make it into a code.
___	*8. refuel	A gas station is a place where people refuel their cars.
___	9. repaid	If you've repaid money, you have paid it back to the lender.
___	10. overgrown	If no one clips or trims the plants in a garden, the garden will become overgrown.
___	11. disrespect	All people should be shown respect, not disrespect.
___	12. intercontinental	An intercontinental flight between New York and London takes six or seven hours.
___	13. confidence	He had confidence in his ability as goalie.
___	14. transportation	She takes public transportation to and from work.
___	15. apartment	My family lives in a two-bedroom apartment.

Name: _____

REVIEW WORDS

___ *16. apart

___ *17. department

___ *18. photograph

___ *19. partly

___ *20. medicine

___ 21. immigrant

___ 22. effortless

___ 23. computer

___ 24. conference

___ 25. layer

Challenge Words

mold, interplanetary, shield, semicircular, unbelievably

Name: _____

1. _____

2. _____

3. _____

4. _____

5. _____

6. _____

7. _____

8. _____

1. _____

2. _____

3. _____

4. _____

5. _____

6. _____

7. _____

8. _____

9. _____

10. _____

_____

Name:
_____

1. _____

2. _____

3. _____

4. _____

5. _____

6. _____

7. _____

8. _____

9. _____

10. _____

_____

Week 25, Day 4

1. _____

2. _____

3. _____

4. _____

5. _____

6. _____

7. _____

8. _____

9. _____

10. _____

_____

Unusual Plurals

NEW WORDS

___	*1. wolves	One wolf howled to the other wolves.
___	*2. oxen	Each ox was strong, so the pair of oxen could pull a heavy wagon.
___	*3. deer	The deer ran gracefully to catch up with all the other deer.
___	*4. radios	All radios were on sale for a week.
___	*5. tomatoes	It was the tastiest tomato of all the tomatoes he'd ever eaten.
___	*6. pianos	The music store had many instruments for sale, including two grand pianos.
___	*7. mice	Field mice live outdoors and eat seeds.
___	*8. leaves	One leaf on the twig had turned orange, while the other leaves were still green.
___	9. knives	The long knife is better for slicing bread than the short knives.
___	10. salmon	First we spotted one salmon, then many salmon, as they swam upstream.
___	11. university	In a university, the teachers of many subjects are gathered in one place.
___	12. reflector	My jacket has a strip of reflector tape so it can be seen in the dark.
___	13. particular	My mother is very particular about the best way to clean the kitchen.

continues

NEW WORDS (continued)

___ 14. interchangeable   The tires of the car and the truck were not interchangeable.

___ 15. source   The source of the Mississippi River is Lake Itasca.

REVIEW WORDS

___ *16. encode

___ *17. subzero

___ *18. cooperating

___ *19. supermarket

___ *20. semisweet

___ *21. refuel

___ 22. overgrown

___ 23. repaid

___ 24. apartment

___ 25. transportation

Challenge Words

error, satellite, vacuum, schedule, preserve

Name: _____

1. _____

2. _____

3. _____

4. _____

5. _____

6. _____

7. _____

8. _____

1. _____

2. _____

3. _____

4. _____

5. _____

6. _____

7. _____

8. _____

9. _____

10. _____

_____

Name:

1. _____

2. _____

3. _____

4. _____

5. _____

6. _____

7. _____

8. _____

9. _____

10. _____

_____

1. _____

2. _____

3. _____

4. _____

5. _____

6. _____

7. _____

8. _____

9. _____

10. _____

_____

Name: _____

More Words with Suffixes

NEW WORDS

___	*1. awareness	Once you gain an awareness of recycling, you can recycle almost everything.
___	*2. wealthy	The wealthy couple generously gave money to the local food bank.
___	*3. youthful	The old man had a youthful appearance.
___	*4. magically	The rabbit seemed to appear magically.
___	*5. ninetieth	After what seemed like the ninetieth attempt, my dad was finally able to fix the broken engine.
___	*6. fortieth	My father gave my mother a surprise party on her fortieth birthday.
___	*7. blindness	There are more ways to prevent and cure blindness than there were 100 years ago.
___	*8. daily	We do daily brain teaser exercises during math class.
___	9. feathery	The horse's mane was so long and sleek, it looked almost feathery in the wind.
___	10. dreamer	He was called a dreamer but grew up to be an inventor.
___	11. telescope	At the science museum, a giant telescope was set up for people to see the night sky.
___	12. undated	I couldn't figure out how old the letter was because it was undated.
___	13. heroes	He was the hero of heroes.

continues

NEW WORDS (*continued*)

____ 14. experiment   The artist liked to experiment with many colors.

____ 15. instruments   The pilot checked all the plane's instruments before taking off.

REVIEW WORDS

____ *16. deer

____ *17. tomatoes

____ *18. pianos

____ *19. radios

____ *20. oxen

____ *21. wolves

____ 22. university

____ 23. salmon

____ 24. particular

____ 25. reflector

Challenge Words

nutritious, remote, criminal, courteous, allergic

Name: _____

1. _____

2. _____

3. _____

4. _____

5. _____

6. _____

7. _____

8. _____

1. _____

2. _____

3. _____

4. _____

5. _____

6. _____

7. _____

8. _____

9. _____

10. _____

_____

Name: _____

1. _____

2. _____

3. _____

4. _____

5. _____

6. _____

7. _____

8. _____

9. _____

10. _____

_____

1. _____

2. _____

3. _____

4. _____

5. _____

6. _____

7. _____

8. _____

9. _____

10. _____

_____

Name: _____

Doubling with Polysyllabic Words

NEW WORDS

____ *1. permitting Weather permitting, the wedding will be held outdoors.

____ *2. preferred The cat preferred to sit by the fire.

____ *3. upsetting The thunderstorm was upsetting to the younger children.

____ *4. gardener The gardener knew the Latin name of every plant in the garden.

____ *5. reconsidering My mom didn't think she wanted a new job, but now she's reconsidering.

____ *6. offered When my friend fell, I offered her a hand up.

____ *7. declared Great Britain declared war on the American colonies when they sought independence.

____ *8. station At the train station, we bought our tickets and walked to the platform.

____ 9. castle A medieval castle usually had a moat to keep out intruders.

____ 10. paragraph For homework we had to write the introductory paragraph.

____ 11. overcoat He wore a sweater and an overcoat.

____ 12. echoes They heard many echoes in the cave, but the echo was the loudest when they all shouted together.

____ 13. practically My younger brother played with his friend around the corner practically every day.

continues

NEW WORDS (continued)

____ 14. examine   We will examine the cells under a microscope.

____ 15. pour   Would you please pour me some orange juice?

REVIEW WORDS

____ *16. youthful

____ *17. magically

____ *18. blindness

____ *19. wealthy

____ *20. daily

____ *21. fortieth

____ 22. feathery

____ 23. heroes

____ 24. experiment

____ 25. undated

Challenge Words

threatened, forbidden, bothering, interrupted, delivered

Week 28, Day 1

Name: _____

1. _____ + _____ = _____

2. _____ + _____ = _____

3. _____

4. _____

5. _____ + _____ = _____

6. _____

7. _____

8. _____

1. _____ + _____ = _____

2. _____ + _____ = _____

3. _____

4. _____

5. _____

6. _____

7. _____ + _____ = _____

8. _____

9. _____

10. _____

_____

Name: _____

1. _____ + _____ = _____

2. _____ + _____ = _____

3. _____

4. _____

5. _____

6. _____

7. _____ + _____ = _____

8. _____

9. _____

10. _____

_____

1. _____ + _____ = _____

2. _____ + _____ = _____

3. _____

4. _____

5. _____

6. _____

7. _____ + _____ = _____

8. _____

9. _____

10. _____

_____

Name:

_____

Review of Syllable Constructions and Divisions

NEW WORDS

____ *1. service   Guide dogs provide a valuable service to people who are blind or partially sighted.

____ *2. item   There was one item on the test that I just couldn't figure out.

____ *3. practice   My friend has soccer practice every Tuesday and Thursday.

____ *4. entire   The little girl was so excited that she skipped the entire way home.

____ *5. beneath   He hid the present beneath his jacket so his mom wouldn't see it.

____ *6. handle   I loved that mug, but the handle broke off.

____ *7. shelter (shel.ter)   ^{VC.CV} After the hurricane, people found shelter in the local school.

____ *8. limit (lim.it)   ^{V C .V} During the toy sale, there was a limit of two games per customer.

____ 9. lion (li.on)   ^{V.V} A female lion does not have a mane.

____ 10. event (e.vent)   ^{V.CV} The final assembly program was a major event in the school year.

____ 11. address (ad.dress)   ^{VC.CCV} We moved when I was four, but I can still remember my old address.

____ 12. underestimated I thought we would lose the game, but I had underestimated our team strength.

continues

NEW WORDS (continued)

____ 13. eagerly

The boy eagerly helped his teacher erase the board.

____ 14. forgotten

Our dog had not forgotten where she buried the bone.

____ 15. spirit

The new student felt the spirit of friendliness in the classroom.

REVIEW WORDS

____ *16. offered

____ *17. station

____ *18. declared

____ *19. upsetting

____ *20. permitting

____ *21. gardener

____ 22. castle

____ 23. echoes

____ 24. overcoat

____ 25. examine

Challenge Words

pioneers, alertness, harvested, attitude, defeated

Name: _____

1. _____

2. _____

3. _____

4. _____

5. _____

6. _____

7. _____

8. _____

1. _____

2. _____

3. _____

4. _____

5. _____

6. _____

7. _____

8. _____

9. _____

10. _____

_____

Name: _____

1. _____

2. _____

3. _____

4. _____

5. _____

6. _____

7. _____

8. _____

9. _____

10. _____

_____

1. _____

2. _____

3. _____

4. _____

5. _____

6. _____

7. _____

8. _____

9. _____

10. _____

_____

Review of Weeks 23, 25, 26, 27, and 28

Week 23

___ *1. microscope

___ *2. department

___ *3. medicine

___ *4. particles

___ *5. telephone

___ 6. layer

___ 7. immigrant

___ 8. universe

___ 9. conference

___ 10. quarter

Week 25

___ *11. supermarket

___ *12. forearm

___ *13. cooperating

___ *14. semisweet

___ *15. injustice

___ 16. disrespect

___ 17. repaid

___ 18. apartment

___ 19. intercontinental

___ 20. confidence

Week 26

___ *21. radios

___ *22. mice

___ *23. leaves

___ *24. tomatoes

___ 25. university

___ 26. knives

___ 27. source

___ 28. reflector

___ 29. interchangeable

___ 30. particular

continues

REVIEW WEEK WORDS (continued)

Week 27

___ *31. daily

___ *32. ninetieth

___ *33. magically

___ *34. fortieth

___ *35. awareness

___ 36. dreamer

___ 37. heroes

___ 38. telescope

___ 39. instruments

___ 40. experiment

Week 28

___ *41. upsetting

___ *42. preferred

___ *43. reconsidering

___ *44. declared

___ *45. gardener

___ 46. paragraph

___ 47. pour

___ 48. echoes

___ 49. examine

___ 50. practically

Challenge Words

Week 23 saxophone, medication, ghost, participate, telegraph

Week 25 mold, semicircular, shield, interplanetary, unbelievably

Week 26 preserve, satellite, schedule, error, vacuum

Week 27 criminal, nutritious, allergic, courteous, remote

Week 28 threatened, forbidden, bothering, delivered, interrupted

1. _____

2. _____

3. _____

4. _____

5. _____

6. _____

7. _____

8. _____

9. _____

10. _____

11. _____

12. _____

13. _____

14. _____

15. _____

1. _____

On intercontinental flights, some jets can be refueled while flying.

2. _____

The astronomy department has a teliscope and other astronomical

_____

instruments that the unaversity is permitting the public to view.

3. _____

We used knifes to cut the semesweet chocolate squares we bought

_____

at the supermarket.

4. _____

With a micrascope, we could examin some practicly invisible particles.

5. _____

The dreamer prefered to think of ordinary life as magicial.

Dictionary and Personal Word List

Dictionary and Personal Word List

Name: _____

A

— absent

— acceptable

— accidentally

— actually

— address

— advantage

— adventure

— advice

— airplane

— alarm

— ambulance

— announce

— apart

— apartment

— applied

— applying

— armies

— article

— artistic

— assistants

— attach

— attendance

— awareness

_____

_____

_____

_____

_____

_____

_____

B

— background

— balance

— beautiful

— belong

— beneath

— blindness

— border

— bowl

— breakable

— broad

— broken

— buffalo

_____

_____

_____

_____

C

— cage

— calm

— camel

— camera

— camping

— capital

— captain's

— capturing

— castle

— centuries

— chapter

— character

— children's

— choice

— collect

— colonial

— comfortable

— computer

— concern

— conference

— confidence

— conflict

— content

— cooperating

Name: _____

___ cotton
___ couldn't
___ county
___ courage
___ crops
___ curious
_____
_____
_____
_____
_____
_____
_____
_____

D

___ daily
___ damaged
___ daughter
___ deal
___ declared
___ deer
___ defining

___ degrees
___ department
___ depth
___ describing
___ details
___ detective
___ dictionary
___ difference
___ dirty
___ discount
___ disposable
___ disrespect
___ distance
___ division
___ double
___ dozen
___ dreamer
_____
_____
_____
_____
_____
_____
_____

_____
_____

E

___ eagerly
___ earn
___ easily
___ echoes
___ effortless
___ encode
___ enemies
___ engineer
___ enormous
___ entire
___ equal
___ evening
___ event
___ examine
___ excellent
___ excitable
___ expensive
___ experience
___ experiment
___ explanation
___ expression

Dictionary and Personal Word List

Name: _____

___ extra
___ extremely

_____

_____

_____

_____

_____

_____

_____

_____

F

___ farther
___ fashion
___ feathery
___ fence
___ fixing
___ flew
___ football
___ forearm
___ forgotten
___ forth
___ fortieth
___ fought

___ furniture
___ furry

_____

_____

_____

_____

G

___ garbage
___ gardener
___ gentle
___ giant's
___ giants'
___ glance
___ goals

_____

_____

_____

H

___ halfway
___ handle
___ heroes
___ hers

___ hidden
___ hiring
___ honey
___ horrible
___ hospital
___ hungrier
___ husband's

_____

_____

_____

I, J

___ I'm
___ immediately
___ immigrant
___ importance
___ improve
___ independent
___ injustice
___ innocent
___ instructions
___ instruments
___ intend
___ interchangeable

Name: _____

___ intercontinental
___ introduce
___ item
___ it's
___ its
___ journey
_____
_____
_____
_____
_____
_____

K
___ kitchen
___ knees
___ knives
___ knock
___ know
_____
_____

L
___ laid
___ layer

___ leaves
___ limit
___ lion
___ low
_____
_____
_____

M
___ magically
___ magnet
___ manager
___ marriage
___ meatless
___ medical
___ medicine
___ metal
___ mice
___ microscope
___ minerals
___ mirror
___ misled
___ misreported
___ motionless
___ mouse

___ muddy
___ muscles
___ musician
_____
_____
_____
_____
_____
_____

N
___ needle
___ ninetieth
___ nonfat
___ normal
___ noticeable
___ nurses'
_____
_____

O
___ o'clock
___ offered
___ operation
___ opportunity

Dictionary and Personal Word List

— opposite
— orange
— ought
— overcoat
— overgrown
— oxen
— _____
— _____
— _____

P

— paid
— painlessly
— palace
— paper
— paragraph
— particles
— particular
— partly
— pattern
— peacefully
— performance
— perhaps
— permission
— permitting

— photograph
— pianos
— piece
— pleasant
— pledge
— pocket
— port
— pour
— practically
— practice
— preferred
— preflight
— preparing
— prerecorded
— present
— prevention
— printed
— promise
— properly
— protection
— proudly
— _____
— _____
— _____

— _____
— _____
— _____
— _____
— _____
— _____

Q, R

— quarter
— radios
— rather
— raw
— rays
— reach
— reasonable
— reconsidering
— reflector
— refuel
— refusing
— relatives
— reliable
— relying
— remove

Dictionary and Personal Word List

Name: _____

___ repaid
___ replying
___ reporter
___ requiring
___ responsibly
___ reusable
___ review
___ roll
___ route
___ royal
_____
_____
_____
_____
_____
_____
_____

S
___ sailor
___ salmon
___ satisfied
___ semisweet
___ sense

___ sensible
___ sentence
___ serious
___ servant
___ service
___ shadow
___ shelter
___ shopping
___ signal
___ silent
___ sister's
___ sisters'
___ situation
___ skidded
___ skin
___ sleepiest
___ slept
___ smoky
___ smoother
___ something
___ sorry
___ source
___ spirit
___ staring
___ station

___ steady
___ steel
___ stomach
___ subzero
___ succeed
___ suggestion
___ superintendent
___ supermarket
___ support
___ supposed to
___ sure
___ surprising
___ surrounded
___ swimmer
___ swimming
___ switches
___ system
_____
_____
_____
_____
_____
_____
_____

Name: _____

_____	__tomorrow	_____
_____	__tongue	_____
_____	__topic	_____
_____	__tough	_____
_____	__trader	
_____	__trainer	**U**
_____	__transport	__uncrowded
_____	__transportation	__undated
_____	__tremendous	__underestimated
	__trotting	__unexplored
T	__truly	__uniform
__table of contents	__trunk	__union
__tank	__turkey	__unit
__tear	__twelve	__united
__telephone	__twenty	__universe
__telescope	__twice	__university
__that'll	_____	__unwrapped
__their	_____	__upsetting
__they've	_____	__upstairs
__thought	_____	_____
__thrill	_____	_____
__throw	_____	_____
__tightly	_____	_____
__tomatoes	_____	_____

V

__valuable

__value

__visit

_____

_____

W

__wagon

__wealthy

__we'd

__welcome

__which

__whisper

__whole

__who's

__wide

__wisest

__wolves

__wore

_____

_____

_____

_____

_____

X, Y, Z

__you're

__yours

__youthful

_____

_____

_____

Spelling References

Name:
_____

Single-syllable Doubling Generalization

IF the base word has

 – one syllable,

 – one vowel,

 – and one consonant after the vowel

AND the suffix begins with a vowel,

THEN double the last consonant.

Examples

stop + ing = stopping   sun + y = sunny

big + est = biggest   hid + en = hidden

Drop e Generalization

IF the base word ends with consonant-**e**

AND the suffix begins with a vowel,

THEN drop **e**.

Examples

ride + ing = riding   brave + est = bravest

write + er = writer   shine + y = shiny

Change y to i Generalization

IF the base word ends with consonant-**y**

AND the suffix begins with any letter except **i**,

THEN change **y** to **i**.

Examples

puppy + es = puppies   happy + ness = happiness

carry + ed = carried   beauty + ful = beautiful

Polysyllabic Doubling Generalization

IF the base word is polysyllabic

   – and ends with one vowel and one consonant

   – and has the accent on the last syllable

AND the suffix begins with a vowel,

THEN double the last consonant.

Examples

begin + ing = beginning   begin + er = beginner

admit + ed = admitted   forgot + en = forgotten

Frequently Misspelled Words

Name:

The phrases in parentheses will help you choose the correct word. Contractions and compound word families are shown on page 188.

A
all ready (*They are all ready.*)
all right
a lot
already (*They've already left.*)

B
because
before
believe
buy (*She will buy a pen.*)

C
cannot
classroom
clothes (*She picked up her clothes.*)
coming
couldn't

D, E, F
Dr.
eight
eighteen
eighteenth
eighty
February
field
first

forth (*back and forth*)
forty
fourteen
fourth (*third and fourth*)
friend

G, H
great-grandmother
guess
halfway
hear (*I can hear you.*)
heard (*He heard a sound.*)

I, J, K
I'm
January
Jr.
know

L, M, N
loose (*The knot came loose.*)
lose (*Don't lose your pen.*)
men's
Miss
Mon.
Mr.
Mrs.
Ms.
ninety

O, P
off
one (*There's one page left.*)
ourselves
paid
people
piece (*piece of pie*)

Q, R, S
quite (*quite beautiful*)
Saturday
school
sense (*common sense*)
something
St. (*Main St.; St. Louis*)
sure

T, U, V
their (*Join their group.*)
there (*There it is.*)
thirty
thought
threw (*She threw the ball.*)
through (*Wind blew through the window.*)
too (*I ran too fast. I like that book, too.*)
touch
truth

Name:

Tuesday
twice
two (*We ate two oranges.*)
used to

W, X, Y, Z
wanted
water

weather (*sunny weather*)
were
what
where
whether (*He asked whether he could go.*)
which
while

whole (*the whole book*)
who's (*Who's absent?*)
whose (*Whose book is this?*)
wind (*The wind blew. Wind up the string.*)
women
would (*Yes, I would.*)

Frequently Misspelled Words

Name:

CONTRACTIONS

n't (not)	's (is, has)	'll (will, shall)	'd (would, had)	've (have)	're (are)	'm (am) 's (us)
aren't	here's	he'll	he'd	I've	they're	I'm
can't	he's	I'll	I'd	you've	we're	let's
couldn't	how's	it'll	she'd	we've	you're	
didn't	it's	she'll	they'd	they've		
doesn't	she's	that'll	we'd			
don't	that's	they'll	who'd			
hadn't	there's	we'll	you'd			
hasn't	what's	you'll				
haven't	where's					
isn't	who's					
mustn't						
shouldn't						
wasn't						
weren't						
won't						
wouldn't						

COMPOUND WORD FAMILIES

no-	any-	some-	every-	-ever
nobody	anybody	somebody	everybody	forever
nowhere	anyone	somehow	everyone	however
	anything	someone	everything	whatever
	anyway	something	everywhere	whenever
	anywhere	sometime		
		sometimes		
		somewhat		
		somewhere		